Falling Outside Eden

First published 2019 by The Hedgehog Poetry Press

Published in the UK by
The Hedgehog Poetry Press
5, Coppack House
Churchill Avenue
Clevedon
BS21 6QW

www.hedgehogpress.co.uk

ISBN: 978-1-9160908-1-1

A CIP Catalogue record for this book is available from the British Library.

Falling Outside Eden

by

Melissa Fu

Contents

I. EDEN

For you: the bigger half of the wishbone,
this garden in the weeds, a sandcastle
with ramparts of shells and kelp.
All, all yours. Will you have them?

THRESHOLD

Until then, I was almost
invisible. Nearly not seen,
unlabelled, unmarked.

In those moments
when I didn't know if the sky
was very large or very small,

when I couldn't tell you my name,
or yours, or the nature of
our acquaintance,

I found something that
almost cradled my cheek
like cottonwood down

that almost stroked my shoulder
blades like sunlight, that almost
felt like home.

That, if listened to
with the soles of my feet,
whispered

be still
count your heartbeats
measure your breaths

And there I was
waiting and
unaware,

tracing my lifeline
with a pine needle
and a jay's feather.

INVITATION TO THE MONSOON

arrive at the dip in the day
everywhere, a lull

unfold differently -
heedless, hushed

assume a hidden dimension
between salt and waves

listen long: the sea bluffs
shingle of shells, poker chip pebbles

bring cinnamon tea and
the chords of no moon at all

CIRCLES

the earth	the sun
the moon	the earth
the mountains	the horizon
the willows	the lake
the wagons	the camp
the dancers	the tree
the stones	the fire
the garlands	the bride
the ring	the finger
the bee	the blossom
the moth	the flame

WE WERE DREAMING OF WATERMELON

of the thump of ripeness
the cracking of green mottled skin
revealing a flush of pink flesh

of drip and slurp and crunch

of hard black-brown seeds
spit far – ten feet, twelve feet –
scattered and dusty

of drip and slurp and crunch

of tiny white seeds, still
nestled in the fruit, swallowed
whole in greedy mouthfuls

of drip and slurp and crunch

of juice running down
cheeks and elbows
leaving sticky trails

of drip and slurp and crunch

of ants, like vultures, itching to
climb carcasses of pale rinds,
waiting to devour any spots

of sweetness left behind

WAKING

Dreams disperse
like prayer flags
faded by sun
unravelled by wind.

Morning gusts
blow bright fancy
into thin-threaded echo

as coloured strands
ascend to become
woven into waking.

II. ENCOUNTERS

We couldn't have known then
the way our feathers would fall
the way we'd lose our convictions
like milk teeth.

PECCADILLOS

Speaking of sins,
once, in Paris, I ate
three ice creams and
a dozen macarons
before lunchtime.

Later, in a parfumerie,
I sprayed samples
until I nearly fainted
in clouds of ginger,
juniper and green grass.

As a parting gesture,
I lost a lover's silk scarf
because the design had
curlicue swirls of pastel,
and I hate pastels.

Worst of all,
when I really
love something,
I have no taste
for irony.

WHAT YOU ASK

If you would know me,
then you would know this:

When you ask me a good question
(by that, I mean a bottomless one),
you spring the trapdoor under my feet
I start tumbling to wonderland,
turning your question over and over,
my hands sounding its depths.

And because it is a good question
(by that, I mean a sharp and gleaming one),
you cleave me from my words
I become mute and swallow silence
chasing discord down dark passageways
my language no longer rising to speech.

As we descend, your riddle and I,
we eye one another, Sphinx-like,
without inscription or solution -
twinned and twirling, two sisters,
one giving birth to the other,
who gives birth to the first.

Knowing this, knowing me,
what is it you would ask?

UPDATE

Since your last visit,

two more red wine stains
have bloomed on the carpet,

another four pieces of wedding china
have shattered on the stone floors,

and the war of the weeds and roses
was a decisive victory for the weeds.

Yes, that is the same layer of dust
you inspected previously,

grown thick and soft with neglect.
I thought of brushing it away,

but it seems a shame to disturb
something that has settled

so beautifully.

LOUDER THAN WORDS

Tell me you don't care that it's late and the day is jagged,
tell me you didn't really come for the book or the cigarettes,
tell me that what has passed doesn't matter (not tonight, anyway),
tell me where you've been; I've been looking for you for years.

Wait.

Don't try to squeeze decades into minutes. Tell me
a story instead, a riddle I can wrap my fingers round,
a poem that I can palm under the table,
a tale that will carry me through the next dry spell,

sing me that song - the one you wrote at midnight
when the city stopped blazing and the cicadas fell silent -
with its sad chords and lyrics lifted from John Donne's poetry,
that's what I want to hear.

No. Don't sing that song (I know it by heart already).

Say you're thinking of raising chickens,
say you've planted radishes and runner beans,
say your 97-year old grandmother still serves tea
in the blue teapot we bought her in Hondo. Say that
sometimes you still go there - to the abandoned
house where we lost your grandma's pith helmet and kissed....

Stop.

Don't say any of that. Not the part about the teapot
and definitely not the part about the pith helmet.
S*hh*, my finger to your lips,
tell me nothing,
don't say
a word.

LIES

The moon is made of cheese.
Cats have nine lives.
Practice makes perfect.

All roads lead to Rome.
Coffee cures a hangover.
Diamonds are forever.

You were stuck in traffic.
You'll stay in touch.
You can't remember.

I don't love you anymore.
No harm was meant.
All is forgiven.

III. FALLING

Every time I look up these days,
something else is making its descent
like rain tracing window panes or
leaves drifting down a stair well.

PROFLIGATE BEAUTY

Every year they do it:
Shower coins of gold
onto the streets,
spend their splendour,
blaze away months
of steady growth in
one clarion bright week,
drop crimson banners
and falling flames,
fill the gutters
with jewels.

And when the tossing,
waving limbs finally
unleave themselves,
only bare arms
remain, with
not even a stitch
left for winter.

STILL LIFE

Outside it is snowing and that is where I want to be.
I want to be there while tree boughs freed of leaves
hold first their own shapes and then the snow.
Then the snow, armful by armful, gatherers up and
reaches back towards the clouds it came from.

You are sleeping. Under thick blankets and dreams
you drift away from a life we once shared.

In the night a stranger is wearing the scarf I lost.
The scarf I lost was whipped away by the winds.
No, it fell because I was following you and I forgot.
And I forgot to notice because the night was mild
and the light was long and you were city blocks away.

On the table, a glass of water evaporates. Drop by drop.
Becomes air again, makes the room heavy with moisture.

There is a playground. There is too much moon.
I can't say if the air is laced with frost. I can't say your name.
your name creaky swings yellowed grass ice-covered puddles
There is a picnic table with flaking paint. There is a basketball court
with faded lines - these edges aren't so clear anymore.

DUST

neglect's partner
arrives invisibly

lays its soft foundations
scatters its scent

between the leaves of letters
in the pages of old books

echo of entropy
tone and timbre blurred away

soul renounced
bereft of body

like the poor
like the passed

with us always

DOORWAY

You stand at the doorway
        I stand at the doorway
the doorway of a house
        where we used to live
that we no longer have no keys for
        I can't unstep that threshold
You leave the door open
        because I leave that door open
because we have no keys so
        something we hadn't thought of
something important
        might still come in
might not be locked out
        standing in the doorway
You look up and see me
        I am waving hello
once again
        or maybe goodbye

PASSAGE

There are so many ways to decay:
fade wilt wither soften rot collapse.
The structure degrades, folds on itself
from the inside or the out, grows smaller.
Bones become pitted, lose calcium.
Skins become thin thinner translucent.

When it rains, the bone aches where it broke,
the fracture leaves legacies of foresight,
bristles, charged and humming,
in tune with all the broken bits,
and all the about to be broken bits,
of the universe.

IV. OUTSIDE

Not all myths end in flames, feathers to cinders.
Some, like Orion, Pegasus, Perseus, rise:
lifting, flying, fading until their joints become stars,
and we redraw their bones with each telling.

VENUS EXITS EAST

Yesterday, Venus faded
from the morning sky.
This is how love leaves:
each dawn a little less shine.
Until one waking, she no longer
holds vigil at your windowsill,
gone to watch over the zenith and nadir
of someone else's love affair.

NOCTURNE

After *Hush*, by David St. John

The way a solo night jazzman serenading the river
releases low trills and slow sighs, shaping and
pulling a supple blue tune from under his fingers
that he hums deep and frequent, until he knows
that the line has found curled winds to ride
and the notes can grow their own echoes;
So I go everywhere, feeding any jukebox
old nickels, sorting the songs from
the songs, to stitch into a cadence of you,
and add from each honkytonk
one more high lonesome lick – the way
a lone rambler's bootsoles carry
the dust from each town.
As you sing low, as if crooning
to an orphan you recover
from the thick morning damp,
the sound tumbles, instead, toward me.
Nothing holds them, those whispers. Not
the arcade of evening. Not the
worn-wired speakers filling the room
with their strains. The songs
swell. Sometimes they call to each other.
Sometimes, we answer;
we weave them together
as water weaves water
under bridges blurred
and melodic, a slow
syncopation
of jazzmen
and night.

ENLIGHTEN

A thread that, caught
on some rock or twig,
unravels as you climb.

A lightening, a layer
unweaving, leaving
strands for crows,

filaments strewn
like cobwebs
limned with dew.

At the peak, nothing
shields your shoulders.
Harsh winds, sun

direct on your skin.
Uncovered, exposed,
elemental.

SOLSTICE

The year's become a candle stub
a taper burnt low, with only a trace
of mornings left to light. I draw close
to the river, walk its banks, ask how
to play out the calendar's coda.

Forgive, says the willow who lost a limb
In April under the weight of too much.
Forgive? The word tastes like chalk and
I wish I hadn't put it in my mouth.
What does it mean? *Only this:*

That when sorrow cloaks the sky and
you lose all appetite for rain and ritual,
visit again the houses you entered first
by sunlight. Go now. On a dry leaf,
on a weak wind, barefoot on cold ground.

That on this, the shortest day coupled
with the longest night, you find solace
in the indifferent rime. Can you accept
numbness when it is the only way
to cross those thresholds?

That however frozen, with no offerings
of clementines and holly, you return
you to yourself, like a lost mitten,
like an orphan's key, like unread ghosts,
waiting to be released. Go now.

THEN WAS OUR EDEN

There we discovered
the taste of new fruit,
drank deep draughts of air,
wore living bodies,

saw who we could be,
if only we dared
claim the names
already our own.

We had to leave
the garden.

Outside,

as riptides polish
seaglass to pebbles,
you sink deep into my
blood and walking bones.

This love grows.
It grows mute.
Like sky and mountain
It becomes what I know.

ACKNOWLEDGEMENTS

With heartfelt gratitude to the readers and editors of the following journals where the noted poems were first published:

'Dust', 'Enlighten' and 'Then was our eden', *A Restricted View From Under the Hedge*; 'Solstice', *The Road to Clevedon Pier;* 'Threshold', 'invitation to the monsoon' and 'circles' *Night Music Journal;* 'Louder than words' and 'Update' *Bitterzoet Magazine;* 'Waking', *Blue Heron Review;* 'Nocturne', *Bare Fiction Magazine;* 'Lies', *Envoi;* 'Profligate Beauty', runner up in Nik Perring's *150 Words Inspired by Trees* Competition; 'Passage' and 'we were dreaming of watermelon' *Firefly Magazine*

I'd also like to thank my fellow writers in the Angles Writing Group, whose friendship and feedback have enriched my poetry, my prose, and my life. Special thanks to Ingrid Jendrzejewski for helping me to find the structure of this pamphlet.

Appreciation to Mark Davidson for making Hedgehog Poetry a community of poetic wonder and to Sue Burge for selecting this pamphlet as the winner of the inaugural Nicely Folded Paper Pamphlet Competition.

Lastly, with love always to Matthew - for reading, believing, and supporting.